e to P

D1328182

DK READERS is a compelling program for beginning readers, designed in conjunction with leading literacy experts, including Dr. Linda Gambrell, Distinguished Professor of Education at Clemson University. Dr. Gambrell has served as President of the National Reading Conference, the College Reading Association, and the International Reading Association.

Beautiful illustrations and superb full-color photographs combine with engaging, easy-to-read stories to offer a fresh approach to each subject in the series. Each DK READER is guaranteed to capture a child's interest while developing his or her reading skills, general knowledge, and love of reading.

The five levels of DK READERS are aimed at different reading abilities, enabling you to choose the books that are exactly right for your child:

Pre-level 1: Learning to read
Level 1: Beginning to read
Level 2: Beginning to read alone
Level 3: Reading alone
Level 4: Proficient readers

The "normal" age at which a child begins to read can be anywhere from three to eight years old. Adult participation through the lower levels is very helpful for providing encouragement, discussing storylines, and sounding out unfamiliar words.

No matter which level you select, you can be sure that you are helping your child learn to read, then read to learn!

DK

LONDON, NEW YORK, MUNICH,
MELBOURNE, AND DELHI

Series Editor Deborah Lock, Penny Smith
Art Editor Jacqueline Gooden
U.S. Editors Elizabeth Hester, John Searcy
Pre-production Francesca Wardell
Jacket Designer Natalie Godwin

Reading Consultant
Linda Gambrell, Ph.D.

First American Edition, 2005
This edition, 2013
Published in the United States by DK Publishing, Inc.
375 Hudson Street, New York, New York 10014

13 14 15 16 17 10 9 8 7 6 5 4 3 2 1
002—192121—July/2013

A catalog record for this book is available
from the Library of Congress

ISBN: 978-1-4654-0944-7 (Paperback)
ISBN: 978-1-4654-0945-4 (Hardcover)

Color reproduction by Colourscan, Singapore
Printed and bound in China by L Rex Printing Co., Ltd.

The publisher would like to thank the following for their kind
permission to reproduce their photographs:
a=above; c=center; b=below; l=left; r=right; t=top

Alamy Images: Comstock Images 22-23; Bruce Coleman Inc 27t;
BSH Stock 14t; Colin Harris/ LightTouch Images 8bl; FLPA 16bl;
gopi 9bcr; Greg Philpott 9bc; Ian Miles/ Flashpoint Pictures 9bl; Ivor
Toms 9br; Lynne Siler/ Focus Group 8br; Mark Sykes 8bcr, 32tc;
Robography 9bcl; Stock Connection Distribution 15b. **Corbis:** Ariel
Skelley 11, 20b; Geoff Moon; Frank Lane Picture Agency 17bcl, 17t;
Kevin Fleming 6t; Kevin Schafer 17bl, 17br, 32cra; Najlah Feanny
28-29; Norbert Schaefer 26c; Scott T. Smith 17bcr; Tom Stewart
30-31. **DK Images:** Philip Dowell 29bc. **Getty Images:** Andy Sacks
12-13; Peter Cade 24-25; Robert Daly 18-19; Yellow Dog
Productions 8-9. **N.H.P.A.:** Ernie Janes 16br. **Zefa Visual Media:**
Masterfile / Kevin Dodge 4-5; Noel Hendrickson 16t.

All other images © Dorling Kindersley
For more information see: www.dkimages.com

Discover more at
www.dk.com

DK READERS

LEARNING
TO READ
pre-level
1

Petting
Zoo

DK

DK Publishing

 What kind of animal

We are at the
petting zoo.

lo you see here?

We are petting
a drowsy donkey.

  donkeys

ear

hoof

We are walking two baby llamas.

llamas

leash

I am brushing a pony's coat.

mane

  ponies

 pigs

I am picking up
a little pink pig.

snout

hoof

hen

chicks

I am carrying a soft yellow chick.

chick

 stick insects

leaf

stick insect

I am holding
a green stick insect.

 frogs

I am watching
a beady-eyed frog.

Ribbit! Ribbit!

toe

It is mealtime now.
I give the woolly lamb
some milk.

 lambs

wool

I am feeding
a hungry rabbit.

ear

carrot

rabbits

This fluffy guinea pig
is nibbling a leaf.

 guinea pigs

whiskers

claws

The white goose wants a snack.

 geese

gosling

bill

feathers

 goats

This long-horned goat is eating his lunch.

horn

29

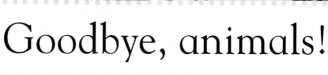 Goodbye, animals!

It's time to go home.

Glossary

Donkey
a small horse-like animal with long ears

Frog
a short animal with long back legs

Goose
a large white bird with a long beak

Llama
a large woolly animal from South America

Stick insect
a long thin insect that looks like a stick

[2]